Native
American
Peoples

APACHE

D. L. Birchfield

Gareth Stevens Publishing
A WORLD ALMANAC EDUCATION GROUP COMPANY

Please visit our web site at: www.garethstevens.com
For a free color catalog describing Gareth Stevens Publishing's list of high-quality books
and multimedia programs, call 1-800-542-2595 (USA) or 1-800-387-3178 (Canada).
Gareth Stevens Publishing's fax: (414) 332-3567.

Library of Congress Cataloging-in-Publication Data

Birchfield, D. L., 1948-
    Apache / by D. L. Birchfield.
        p. cm. — (Native American peoples)
    Summary: A discussion of the history, culture, and contemporary life of the
Apache Indians.
    Includes bibliographical references and index.
    ISBN 0-8368-3664-2 (lib. bdg.)
    1. Apache Indians—History—Juvenile literature. 2. Apache Indians—Social
life and customs—Juvenile literature. [1. Apache Indians.] I. Title. II. Series.
    E99.A6B56   2003
    979.004'972—dc21   2002191116

First published in 2003 by
Gareth Stevens Publishing
A World Almanac Education Group Company
330 West Olive Street, Suite 100
Milwaukee, WI 53212 USA

Produced by Discovery Books
Project editor: Valerie J. Weber
Designer and page production: Sabine Beaupré
Photo researcher: Rachel Tisdale
Native American consultant: Robert J. Conley, M.A., Former Director of Native American
    Studies at Morningside College and Montana State University
Maps and diagrams: Stefan Chabluk
Gareth Stevens editorial direction: Mark Sachner
Gareth Stevens art direction: Tammy Gruenewald
Gareth Stevens production: Jessica L. Yanke

Photo credits: Native Stock: cover, pp. 7 (bottom), 17 (both), 18 (top), 20, 21, 22, 24 (both), 25,
26; Peter Newark's American Pictures: pp. 4, 9, 10, 11, 13, 14, 15, 19; North Wind Picture
Archives: pp. 6, 8; Corbis: pp. 5, 7 (top), 12, 16, 18 (bottom), 23 (both); Joanna Pinneo: 27.

Printed in the United States of America

1 2 3 4 5 6 7 8 9 07 06 05 04 03

Cover: A beaming Apache man with traditional feathers carries his child.

Contents

Chapter 1: Origins 4

Chapter 2: History 6

Chapter 3: Traditional Way of Life 14

Chapter 4: Today 22

Time Line 28

Glossary 29

More Resources 30

Things to Think About and Do 31

Index 32

Words that appear in the glossary are printed in **boldface** type the first time they appear in the text.

Origins

This Jicarilla Apache man was photographed in 1904 by Edward S. Curtis.

The Apaches' homelands once stretched from northern Mexico to Colorado.

Land of the Apaches

The Apaches are a North American Native people whose historic homeland included a large portion of today's U.S. Southwest and northern Mexico. Today, tens of thousands of Apaches live in the United States, mostly in Oklahoma, New Mexico, and Arizona.

Little is known for certain about how the Apaches and other Native Americans got to North America. In most Native cultures, stories of their people's origins have been told for generations. Apache origin stories tell of heroes coming from beneath the earth, led by Changing Woman (sometimes called White-painted Woman), who had magic powers. Helped by a spirit known as Life Giver, Changing Woman and other heroes fought monsters and made the earth safe for humans. The stories have great significance for Apache culture.

Apaches on the Move

Scientists differ in their theories about how and when Native Americans arrived in North America. Some think Indians came from Asia and migrated to North America thousands of years ago, during the last Ice Age. They suggest

In New Mexico, Apaches occupied land that had been abandoned by the ancient Mogollon people. These Mogollon ruins are at Gila Cliff Dwellings National Monument in New Mexico.

that Native Americans crossed a landmass across today's Bering Strait between North America and Asia — a landmass that does not exist anymore. Others think they came from across the seas.

Most scholars believe Apaches migrated from the north, arriving in the Southwest region of today's Arizona and New Mexico perhaps as early as A.D. 800 or 900. Others think the Apaches might have arrived in the Southwest after the great **drought** of the late 1300s. The drought caused ancient civilizations of the region, including a people called the Mogollon, to abandon most of the area and move their farming villages near big rivers, where they could rely on getting water. The Apaches would have moved in and replaced them.

Apache Words

Apache	Pronunciation	English
gah	gah	rabbit
beso	bay so	coin
cho	choh	large
chaa	chah	beaver
kih	key	building
tu	too	water
doo	doh	spring
nada	nah dah	corn

The Apache Language

The name Apache derives from a Zuni Pueblo Indian word meaning "enemy." The Apaches call themselves *Dene*, meaning "The People." The Apache language has six **dialects**: Chiricahua, Jicarilla, Kiowa-Apache, Lipan, Mescalero, and Western Apache.

Chapter 2

History

Life in the Southwest

Before the Spanish began exploring the Southwest in the 1540s, the Eastern Apaches were the lords of the southern Great Plains, with its large herds of buffalo. Mainly a trading people, the Plains Apaches held large annual trade fairs with the Pueblo Indians of New Mexico at the eastern edge of the Great Plains. For several weeks each fall, Apaches from all across the southern Plains traded their buffalo meat and hides to the Pueblos in exchange for corn and pottery.

It has been estimated that there were once more than 70 million buffalo on the Great Plains. The buffalo, and many other animals, including elk and deer, provided for many of the Plains Apaches' needs.

The Western Apaches Adapt

For the Western Apaches, however, west of the Rio Grande, there were no buffalo herds, only a rugged, desert wasteland that no one else wanted. Here, the Apaches proved themselves one of the most **adaptable** people in the world. They discovered and harvested the few food plants of the landscape, such as mescal.

Since the land provided so little food, the Apaches had to spread thinly across the land, breaking up into small, independent units of related families.

During most of the year, the Eastern Plains Apaches hunted and traveled together in similar units. Neither the Eastern nor the Western Apaches formed any kind of national government that other nations could do business with. This situation made it impossible for the Spanish, Mexicans, and Americans who later came to the region to enter into **treaties** with the whole Apache Nation.

Mescal was made from the bulb of an agave plant, dug from the ground and stripped to its heart.

Mescal, Food of the Desert

Apaches harvested mescal in May and June. At the center of this large plant was the heart, a large white bulb 2 or 3 feet (60 to 90 centimeters) around. About 2,000 pounds (900 kilograms) of mescal would be cooked at one time in the bottom of a big pit lined with stones, on which fires were built. The food's flavor was similar to molasses, with a syrupy, sticky, fibrous texture. It could also be dried in thin strips, making a food source that would last a long time.

Dried mescal was carried in leather pouches by Apache warriors for trail food. It was lightweight and would last a long time without spoiling.

The Spanish and Mexican Eras

Beginning with Francisco de Coronado in the 1540s, Spanish explorers in the sixteenth century left accounts of the annual Apache trade fairs with the Pueblo Indians. When the Spanish settled New Mexico in 1598, however, they imposed taxes on the Pueblos that left them without anything to trade with the Apaches. The annual Apache trade fairs came to an end, forever changing the **economy** of the Plains Apaches.

Another huge change came when the Comanche Nation migrated south. Beginning in the early 1700s, they traveled from Wyoming to the southern Great Plains because they wanted to control the southern buffalo herds. Within a few decades, the Comanches drove the Plains Apaches from the area. About 1724, the Comanches and Apaches fought a great battle on the Plains, which the Apaches lost. Most of the Plains Apaches were driven

When the Spanish entered the Southwest, they forced the Indians to work for them. Indian life in the region would never be the same.

Francisco de Coronado, in the 1540s, was the first European to meet the Plains Apaches and the Pueblo Indians of New Mexico. He was disappointed that he didn't find the gold he was looking for.

west, into the mountains of New Mexico. Only two Apache tribes were able to stay on the buffalo plains. The Lipan Apaches stayed south of the Comanches, in far south Texas. The Kiowa-Apaches allied with the Kiowa tribe on the Plains.

Cattle Raids

No longer able to hunt buffalo on Comanche land, the other Plains Apaches soon looked for new sources of food. Soon their whole economy changed to one based on raiding Spanish ranches for horses and cattle to use as food. By the time Mexico gained its independence from Spain, in 1821, Apache raiding was a serious problem in northern Mexico (which included the present-day U.S. states of Arizona and New Mexico).

> The supplying of drink [whiskey] to the Indians will be a means of gaining their goodwill, discovering their secrets, calming them so they will think less of [engaging in] hostilities, and . . . will oblige them to recognize their dependence upon us more directly.
>
> *Bernardo de Galvez, 1786, Spanish Viceroy of Mexico*

> I do not think you will keep the peace. . . . [Y]ou tell me we can stay in our mountains and our valleys. . . . We want nothing but to live in peace. But I do not believe you will allow us to remain on the lands we love.
>
> I warn you, if you try to move us again, war will start once more; it will be a war without end, a war in which every Apache will fight until he is dead.
>
> *Apache chief Cochise to U.S. General O. O. Howard, who had promised the Apaches in 1872 that they could stay in peace on their own land. That promise died with Cochise.*

Apaches were masters at blending in with their environment. They could disappear in the desert and be nearly impossible to find and then suddenly appear to spring an ambush.

The Americans Arrive

In 1848, the United States won a war with Mexico, claiming much of the Apache homeland, including Arizona and New Mexico, which previously belonged to its southern neighbor. Americans began pouring into the region, causing problems for the Apaches — the Americans had little respect for Apache rights to the land.

The End of an Era

Over the next forty years, the Apache groups were rounded up and forced onto reservations. Many Apaches fought against U.S. government troops in

Cochise (1812 – 1874)

Cochise was widely respected as both a war leader and a voice for peace. When he died, he was trying to find a way for his people to live peacefully with the Americans.

Cochise became the most famous Apache war chief during the 1860s. By age twenty-three, he was a war leader of the Chiricahua Apaches. He quickly gained fame for his daring raids on Mexican ranches and towns. When Americans entered the Southwest, Cochise tried to stay at peace with them. In 1861, however, Lieutenant George Bascom accused Cochise of raiding in the United States and arrested him, even though Cochise had come to talk under a white flag of truce. Cochise escaped and for ten years led Apache warriors against U.S. troops in a bloody war. He signed a peace treaty in 1872 and lived peacefully until his death in 1874.

defense of their homelands. By the 1880s, however, only some Western Apaches remained outside the reservation system. Even those Apaches confined to the reservations often left to wage war in protest over the overcrowding, sickness, and poor food on the reservations.

Finally, in 1886, Geronimo and his small band of followers became the last Apaches to surrender. They were sent to Florida as prisoners of war. Open hostilities between Apaches and Americans came to an end and the reservation era began.

Reservation Life

When the Indian wars were over, the U.S. government used the reservation system to try to force Indians to adopt white values. It was a grim time for the Apache people and their culture.

Mescalero Apaches in 1919 on the Mescalero reservation in New Mexico. It would be many years before the Mescaleros began to recover from the harsh conditions of the early reservation years.

> Take stones and ashes and thorns and, with some scorpions and rattlesnakes thrown in, dump the outfit on stones, heat the stones red-hot, set the United States Army after the Apaches, and you have San Carlos.
>
> *Daklugie, nephew of Geronimo, describing San Carlos reservation*

The change to reservation life was very difficult. Poverty, lack of jobs, despair, and poor food caused serious health problems. Apache populations declined at alarming rates. The population of the Jicarilla Apaches, for example, dropped from 995 in 1905 to only 588 in 1920. By 1920, nearly 90 percent of the Jicarilla children suffered from tuberculosis, a serious lung disease.

It was one of the worst periods in American history for Native Americans, a time when Indians did not have many rights, not even freedom of religion. The government was determined to end Indian culture and make Indians just like everyone else, a process called **acculturation**.

Apaches Taking Control

These attitudes began to change in the 1930s when Congress passed the Indian Reorganization Act, which allowed the Apaches

Apache children were taken from their families and sent away to harsh boarding schools where they were forbidden to speak their language and dress in Apache clothing.

and other Indian tribes to form tribal governments again. It was not until 1978, however, that the U.S. government passed the American Indian Religious Freedom Act.

Other laws since then have made it easier for tribal governments to operate businesses. Apache tribes have taken advantage of these changes and today are working to try to improve the lives of their people.

Traditional Way of Life

Traditional Economy

As European-Americans moved onto Native American lands, Indian tribes were forced to adapt dramatically. One of the most remarkable adaptations was how the Apaches shifted their economy from one based on hunting buffalo to one based on raiding Spanish ranches. Apaches became so successful at it that the Spanish in northern Mexico complained that they were practically working for the Apaches.

Lightning-Quick Raids

The Spanish worked all year raising herds of horses, cattle, sheep, and mules. Then, suddenly, the Apaches would sweep down from the north and steal them.

Apache raids sometimes occurred hundreds of miles

An Apache warrior traveled light. Whether on foot or on horseback, Apaches skillfully made their way over the rugged, mountainous terrain of the Southwest.

Apaches became the most skillful raiders in the history of North America. No one knew when or where they would strike, and trying to catch them was nearly impossible.

into Mexico. The raiders often went on foot to their target, traveling through the most rugged, isolated terrain, avoiding contact with anyone and maintaining the element of surprise.

Striking quickly, the Apaches moved the stolen livestock northward at a pace that amazed their pursuers. If the pursuers got too close, some of the Apaches laid ambushes for them, while others continued herding the livestock northward. Once they had reached their home territory, they divided up the livestock and then scattered into the vastness of the landscape, in small groups again, making it virtually impossible for the Spanish, and later for the Mexicans, to pursue them farther. Apache raiding virtually halted the advance of Spanish settlement northward from Mexico.

An Apache bride, dressed for her wedding day. Apache women are a source of strength for their people, respected for their knowledge and hard work.

Apache raiding was so successful that they had very little reason to attempt to become farmers or ranchers. Even by the late 1800s, the United States had trouble convincing the Apaches to farm or ranch.

Traditional Life

Apache traditional culture is matrilineal, meaning that a family tree is traced through the mother's family. When an Apache man married, he went to live with his wife's family and her relatives. Children of the marriage automatically belonged to the wife's **clan**.

An Apache mother-in-law was forbidden to talk to the husband of her daughter. This helped to avoid conflict in the household between a husband and his mother-in-law.

Apaches lived and traveled most of the year in small units of related families, with little traditional formal government. The group was led by someone who was chosen by the others. A leader could lose that position by making foolish decisions or putting the group in danger.

Traditional Crafts

Apache women were skilled at making a kind of basket called a twined **burden** basket. To make them, they coiled reeds and grasses into stout containers to carry nuts and roots. They also made sandals from mescal fibers.

Many of the Apache crafts fell into disuse during the reservation era when the United States established trading houses for the Apaches. They became dependent upon pots and pans and other manufactured goods, instead of their own handiwork. However, baskets and sandals are still made today and are sold in the tribal gift shops.

Apache basket making is a fine art. The baskets are not only beautiful but practical as well. Apache sandals made from mescal fibers were perfectly suited to the desert.

Apache Housing

Eastern Apaches lived in tepees made of buffalo hides, even after they lost the buffalo plains to the Comanches and had to trade with other Indians to get the hides. Western Apaches, however, invented a structure, called a wickiup, that was perfect for their land. Branches were woven together into a round frame and then covered with desert bushes and leaves. Providing shade in the desert heat, the wickiup could be built quickly, with materials readily at hand, and then quickly abandoned, making the Apaches highly **mobile**. It was also nearly invisible because it blended in with the other bushes so well, making an Apache camp hard to find.

Apache Childhood

Apache children began training in how to survive in their harsh land as soon as they were old enough to walk. Each morning, an Apache elder in the camp would wake the children at sunrise and send them running to the top of a hill and back. As they grew older, they were required to carry a mouthful of water all the way without losing any.

Apache girls played with dolls made of corn husks. The dolls are dressed in leather clothing.

On summer mornings, the children would also be made to swim in the ice-cold mountain streams. On winter mornings, they would be made to roll naked in the snow.

By the time Apache children were teenagers, they had learned to withstand cold, heat, hunger, and thirst that few other humans could endure. They were so **agile** that they could run through the rough terrain of their landscape farther and faster than soldiers mounted on horseback.

Apache babies on cradle boards. The cradle boards left the mother free to perform her work while keeping the babies safe.

Apache chief Antonio Maria with his family in 1897. The family is dressed in their finest clothing for the photograph.

A Nation of Athletes

This training produced some the most exceptional **guerrilla warfare** fighters in history. Even as old men, Apache warriors such as Geronimo were superior athletes to the young soldiers who tried to catch them.

For Apache children — and for many adults — foot races were by far the most important of the Apache sports. Men competed against men, women against women, and children against children. Today, this tradition continues as an important part of annual Apache gatherings, most notably among the Jicarilla Apaches in northern New Mexico and the Mescalero Apaches in southeastern New Mexico.

Apache Beliefs

Traditional Apache life includes a belief in a Creator, the Life Giver, who might respond to prayers and aid in dealing with problems. Through ceremonies and prayers, some Apache men and women sought a variety of powers. Some of those powers included the ability to know what was happening at a distance, the power to surprise and defeat an enemy, the power to make the wind blow to create a dust storm to hide from an enemy, and the power to make the horses more gentle. These Apaches became spiritual leaders, whom others consulted.

Ceremonial grounds on the White Mountain Apache reservation in Arizona. The traditional dances performed on the ceremonial grounds help preserve a sense of community in Apache culture.

Death, Be Not Named

Apaches never talked about death and never referred to dead people by name. If death was mentioned during the preparations for a war party, the war party would be canceled. Upon the death of a parent, the children's names would be changed so they would not have to recall how the parent had used their name.

> We had no churches, no religious organizations, no sabbath day, no holidays, and yet we worshipped. Sometimes the whole tribe would assemble to sing and pray; sometimes in a smaller number, perhaps only two or three. . . . Sometimes we prayed in silence; sometimes each one prayed aloud; sometimes an aged person prayed for all of us.
>
> *Geronimo in his book,* Geronimo's Story of His Life

Apache dancers perform the Mountain Spirit Dance in Gallup, New Mexico.

When an Apache died, the body was buried as quickly as possible and the camp was moved. It was believed that illness could be spread by viewing the body or by touching that person's possessions. Everything that person owned was hastily buried with the body.

Apaches also avoided the topic of owls, which they believed were the ghosts of dead people. An owl's hooting caused serious concern in an Apache camp. There were no jokes in the culture regarding owls and no stories about them. Like death, owls were a topic to be avoided.

Today, important Apache ceremonies continue to be performed on the reservations, including the Apache Fire Dance and the Mountain Spirit Dance, which celebrate the continuation of Apache culture.

Today

Literature and the Arts

Apaches have made important contributions to Native American scholarship, literature, and the arts. Jicarilla Apache scholar Veronica E. Velarde Tiller became the first Apache to write a scholarly history of her people, titled *The Jicarilla Apache Tribe,* which concentrates on the problems her people have faced in the twentieth century.

A painted hide by Apache artist Joseph Skywolf. Hide paintings were sometimes used to record historic events by the tribe.

White Mountain Apache poet Roman C. Adrian's poetry has appeared in many publications, including *The Remembered Earth.* The first major collection of Native literature, this book was published in the late 1960s and is widely used in college courses in Native American literature. The late Chiricahua Apache poet Blossom Haozous published traditional Apache stories in both the Apache language and English, including Apache origin stories. In contrast, Jicarilla Apache creative writers Stacey Velarde and Carson Vicenti write stories about modern life, revealing the problems and joys of being an Indian in today's world.

Mescalero Apache Lorenzo Baca is among the most talented creative artists, working in video, sculpture, art, storytelling, and acting. His "round poems" are circle poems, cleverly constructed and fun to read.

A World-Famous Artist

By far the most famous Apache artist, Chiricahua Apache sculptor Alan Houser (1914–1994) received worldwide recognition for his work in marble, bronze, wood, and stone. Houser became famous for his large sculptures, many now in the permanent collections of museums throughout the world. His work won many awards, including the Prix de West Award of the National Cowboy Hall of Fame.

Apache sculptor Alan Houser with one of his large sculptures, in bronze.

Geronimo

Geronimo was not only the most famous Apache war leader and medicine man, but he is also the most famous Apache author. To a translator and a secretary, he dictated *Geronimo's Story of His Life*, one of the most widely read books written by any Indian. He had become so famous by that time that his appearance at the St. Louis World's Fair in 1905, while he was still a prisoner of war, created a sensation. At the World's Fair, he sold photos of himself for ten cents each. He died in prison of pneumonia at Fort Sill, Oklahoma, in 1909.

Apache leader Geronimo (right) with three of his warriors, in Arizona in the 1880s. Geronimo and his Chiricahua band were not allowed to remain in Arizona.

The Western Apaches

This statue overlooks the San Carlos Apache golf course in Arizona. The San Carlos Apaches are attempting to increase their income from tourists.

Home to about seven thousand Western Apaches today, the San Carlos Apache Reservation is one of the poorest places in the United States. The tribe lost most of what little farmland was available when part of the reservation was flooded following the building of the Coolidge Dam in 1930. In recent years, tribal members have made some income by mining **semiprecious** stones such as peridot and by a limited amount of farming. Tourists also come to the reservation to hunt, fish, play golf, or gamble.

Salt River Canyon on the San Carlos Apache reservation in Arizona. Most of San Carlos is harsh, arid land similar to that shown here.

Tribes of the Fort Apache Reservation

The Fort Apache Reservation in eastern Arizona is home to the Coyotero Apaches and also includes the Cibeque and White Mountain Apaches, a total population of about nine thousand. Originally, the reservation contained the largest forest of ponderosa pine trees in the world, but American logging companies were allowed to cut the trees, with very little benefit to the Apaches.

In 1954, the tribe founded the Fort Apache Recreational Enterprise, leading to much economic activity, including building a ski area. The mountains, lakes, and fishing streams lure tourists and their money, boosting tribal income. Farming and cattle raising are also important. The most successful tribal business, however, has been its casino, which lures gamblers by the thousands. The casino doubled in size in 1995.

A young Apache girl on horseback at the Fort Apache reservation.

Apache reservations in Arizona, New Mexico, and Oklahoma.

Mount Graham

Mount Graham, in eastern Arizona, is a **sacred** site for the San Carlos Apaches. In 1988, Congress allowed the University of Arizona, the German Max Planck Institute, the Italian Arcetri Observatory, and the Vatican to build telescopes on Mount Graham. The San Carlos Apache Tribal Council has tried in both the U.S. Congress and the courts to stop the construction. Despite studies that show Mount Graham to be a poor place for using telescopes, in May 2001, a U.S. district judge in Arizona allowed construction to continue on Mount Graham.

The Eastern Apaches

In 1936, the Kiowa-Apaches in western Oklahoma joined with the Kiowas to form a business council for the tribes. Today, the two tribes operate many programs for their people, including health care and educational programs for the children.

Until the 1930s, the Mescalero Apaches of southeastern New Mexico had leased their land to white ranchers for cattle grazing. They then began their own cattle-raising operation, increasing tribal revenue from $18,000 to $101,000 during their first three years. In 1963, the Mescaleros bought a nearby ski area. Since then, they have turned it into a year-round tourist attraction, with a large hotel, tennis courts, restaurants, and a golf course.

An Eastern Apache traditional drummer and singer. The drum is at the very heart of traditional Apache dances.

In northern New Mexico, the Jicarilla Apaches benefited from the discovery of oil on their reservation in the 1950s. By the 1990s, tribal revenue from the oil was $11 million a year. In the 1980s, Jicarilla parents began getting elected to their school board and demanding better education for their children. In 1988, the Jicarilla school district was chosen New Mexico School District of the Year.

Apaches Now and in the Future

Apaches on all the reservations have made great strides in recent decades to overcome the difficulties that threatened their existence as a people. Their population is now increasing and is in the tens of thousands. The survival of their people, and their culture, is a **testament** to their strength. They still face many problems, but they are facing those challenges and looking to the future with hope for a better life for their people.

The Sunrise Ceremony

A young Apache woman's **puberty** ceremony, called *Na'ii'ees*, or the "Sunrise Ceremony," is a **ritual** portrayal of the Apache origin story. The ceremony requires a day of preparation, including a sweat bath, a gift of food to relatives, presentation of the girl by a **medicine man**, and a ceremonial dance. She also runs four laps to represent the four stages of her life. For four days after the ceremony, the girl is considered holy. She is believed to take on the powers of Changing Woman, from the Apache origin story, with power to cure the sick and bring rain.

An Apache girl running laps around ceremonial grounds.

Time Line

800–900	Period when Apaches might have migrated into the Southwest from the north.
1275–1300	Severe, prolonged drought in the Southwest causes ancient civilizations to abandon most of the land. Apaches might have migrated into the region after this time.
1540s–90	Spanish expeditions of Francisco de Coronado and others explore the Southwest, leaving accounts of the Apaches.
1598	Spanish settle New Mexico permanently and disrupt trade relations between Apaches and Pueblo Indians.
early 1700s	The Comanche migration to the Southern Plains from Wyoming pushes most Plains Apaches off the plains, except for the Kiowa-Apaches and the Lipan Apaches.
about 1724	Apaches lose great battle with Comanches for control of the southern Plains.
1848	U.S. war with Mexico ends; Southwest becomes U.S. territory.
1850s–86	The Apaches fight wars with the United States.
1870s–80s	Most Apaches are confined to reservations.
1886	Geronimo surrenders, is sent to Florida as prisoner of war, along with 468 other Apaches.
1887	Kiowa-Apache lands in Indian Territory are opened to American settlers.
1934	Apache tribal governments are formed under Indian Reorganization Act.
1950s	Oil is discovered on the Jicarilla Reservation in New Mexico.
1954	Fort Apache Recreation Enterprise is started.
1963	Mescalero Apache tribe buys ski area to make into resort.
1994	San Carlos Apache tribe opens casino in Arizona.
2001	A judge in Arizona allows telescope construction to continue on Mount Graham.

Glossary

acculturation: the process of forcing one group to adopt the culture — the language, lifestyle, and values — of another.

adaptable: able to change to suit new conditions or surroundings.

agile: able to move and react quickly and easily.

burden: a load; something that is carried.

clan: a group of related families.

dialect: a type of language that is spoken in a particular area or by a particular group of people.

drought: a long period of little rain.

economy: the way a country or people produces, divides up, and uses its goods and money.

guerrilla warfare: a kind of war in which small groups of people make lightning-quick, surprise attacks.

medicine man: a spiritual or religious leader.

mobile: able to move easily.

puberty: the time of physical changes in the body when a girl becomes a woman or a boy becomes a man, usually during the early teenage years.

ritual: a system of special ceremonies.

sacred: having to do with religion or spirituality.

semiprecious: less valuable than gems such as diamonds, rubies, and emeralds.

testament: proof.

treaty: an agreement among two or more nations.

More Resources

Web Sites:

impurplehawk.com/index.html An award-winning website including Apache music, photos, and information on many aspects of Apache life.

www.desertusa.com Contains list of sites about Apache culture.

Videos:

American Experience: Geronimo and the Apache Resistance. WGN Boston, 1993.

Books:

Bial, Raymond. *The Apache.* Marshall Cavendish, 2000.

Burks, Brian. *Runs with Horses.* Harcourt, 1995.

Hoyt-Goldsmith, Diane, and Lawrence Migdale (photographer). *Apache Rodeo.* Holiday House, 1995.

Santella, Andrew. *The Apache* (True Books: American Indians). Children's Press, 2001.

Stanley, George Edward, and Meryle Henderson (illustrator). *Geronimo: Young Warrior* (Childhood of Famous Americans). Aladdin, 2001.

Things to Think About and Do

Buffalo = Horses + Cattle?

The ranches in the Apaches' homeland were established without their permission. Why might Apaches think of horses and cattle on the white men's ranches as a substitute for buffaloes on the plains? Write a paragraph explaining what you think.

Tepees and Wickiups

Draw a picture of what an Apache camp might have looked like. How would an Eastern Apache camp, with its tepees, look different from a Western Apache camp, with its wickiups?

Schooled Away from Home

What kind of problems do you think an Apache child might have at a faraway, U.S. government, military-style boarding school, and how would life be different at an ordinary school near home?

Index

American Indian Religious Freedom Act, 13

Baca, Lorenzo, 22
baskets, 16-17
beliefs, 20-21
boarding schools, 13
buffalo, 6, 8, 9

casinos, 25
childhood, 18
Chiricahua Apache, 11, 22, 23
Cochise, 10, 11
Comanches, 8
Coronado, Francisco de, 8, 9

dances, 21

family life, 16, 18
foot races, 19
Fort Apache Reservation, 25

gambling, 24, 25
Geronimo, 11, 19, 21, 23

Haozous, Blossom, 22
hide paintings, 22
homes (wickiup), 17
horse and cattle raiding, 9, 14-15
Houser, Adrian, 23
housing, 17

Indian Reorganization Act, 12-13

Jicarilla Apaches, 4, 12, 19, 22, 27

Kiowa-Apaches, 9, 26

language, 4
Lipan Apaches, 9
loss of lands, 10, 24

mescal, 6, 7
Mescalero Apaches, 12, 19, 22, 26

origin story, 4

Pueblo Indians, 6, 8

reservations, 10-11, 12, 24, 25
Roman, Adrian C., 22

San Carlos Apache Reservation, 12, 13, 24, 25
sandals, 17
Skywolf, Joseph, 22
Spanish settlement, 8, 15
Sunrise Ceremony, 27

treaties, 7, 11

Velarde, Stacey, 22
Velarde, Veronica E., 22
Vicenti, Carson, 22

White Mountain Apache, 22